You'll Never Know

You'll Never Know
Drawing and Random Interference

Jeni Walwin and Henry Krokatsis

with contributions by

James Flint
Janna Levin
Sally O'Reilly

HAYWARD GALLERY TOURING
South Bank Centre, London

Published on the occasion of *You'll Never Know: Drawing and Random Interference*, a Hayward Gallery Touring exhibition from the South Bank Centre, London, on behalf of Arts Council England

Exhibition tour:

25 March – 18 June 2006	Harris Museum and Art Gallery, Preston
29 July – 24 September	Glynn Vivian Art Gallery, Swansea
30 September – 19 November	The Lowry, Salford
1 December – 7 January 2007	New Art Gallery, Walsall
13 January – 25 February	Tullie House Museum and Art Gallery, Carlisle

Exhibition curated by Jeni Walwin and Henry Krokatsis
Exhibition organised by Roger Malbert, with Henrike Ingenthron and Niamh Clancy

Book design: Valle Walkley
Art Publisher: Caroline Wetherilt
Publishing Co-ordinator: James Dalrymple
Sales Manager: Deborah Power
Printed in Italy by Graphicom

Cover: Richard Long, *Untitled*, 2005
Frontispiece: Sessō Tōyō, *Haboku-style landscape*, Muromachi period, 15th Century. Hanging scroll painting

Published by Hayward Gallery Publishing, South Bank Centre, London SE1 8XX, UK
www.hayward.org.uk

ISBN 1 85332 254 7

Hayward Gallery Publishing titles are distributed outside North and South America by Cornerhouse Publications, 70 Oxford Street, Manchester M1 5NH (tel. +44 (0)161 200 1503; fax. +44 (0)161 200 1504; email: publications@cornerhouse.org; www.cornerhouse.org/publications).

CONTENTS

carbon deposits from burning rags

PREFACE

Drawing is conventionally conceived as an intentional act –
the deliberate and to some degree skilful application of marks
on a surface (usually paper). However, avant-garde strategies
for disrupting the artist's conscious aim and introducing unexpected effects have been deployed in modern art since Dada.
This book and the exhibition to which it relates explore some
manifestations of that impulse to subvert or interrupt the
measured performance of mark-making in contemporary art.
The idea originated in a discussion about forms of printmaking
where an element of unpredictability is implicit. Various
primitive, ingenious or whimsical procedures for introducing
chance into the process of image-making then suggested
themselves. The precedents include Yves Klein's body paintings
and prints, Rebecca Horn's mechanical drawing devices,
Andy Warhol's 'Rorschach' paintings and of course the drips
and splashes of Abstract Expressionism.

The curators of the exhibition, Jeni Walwin and Henry
Krokatsis, share a common interest in this territory, though
with different emphases: the former is particularly concerned
with performative and process-based work, the latter, an artist
himself, focuses more on chance as an essential dimension
of art and life. Their dialogue in this book introduces the
salient issues, and sets them in the historical context of Eastern
spiritual practice, emphasising the serious purpose underlying
what is ostensibly a playful approach to the creative act.

Their introduction is followed by three short essays by
writers with quite different perspectives, exploring the
implications of chance in gambling, quantum physics and art.
This book is not a conventional catalogue and only a few of the

artists and works in the associated exhibition are represented here. They do, however, encompass the full range of approaches, from the purely conceptual to the wholly material, from mechanical chance to the spontaneous manipulation of natural substances.

The proliferation of ideas in Keith Tyson's instructions/ proposals for the production of artworks subverts the notion of creative necessity, and a similar fertility is evident in John Wood and Paul Harrison's 36 actions using a variety of objects and materials to make drawings in a three-dimensional space. Rebecca Horn's *Pencil Mask* could be seen as a precursor to performative practices where the actions of the body are central to the creation of the image. An unorthodox use of the body also features in the drawings that Claude Heath made while blindfolded, where the sense of touch replaces the traditional relationship between hand and eye.

Stephen Cripps's drawings collect traces of the performances in which he activated found machinery and manipulated volatile substances. Working with fire and explosives leads inevitably to unpredictable results, giving chance full reign. This fascination with elemental forces is apparent in Dave Farnham's film of a lighted fuse delineating an interior space and in the smoke drawings of Henry Krokatsis. Natural elements are instrumental in determining the final image in a number of other works: the wind in Tim Knowles's *Tree Drawings* and the sun in Anne Bean's tracing of shadows over time. The minute disturbances of dust particles are recorded live in Damien Roach's video; and organic matter is the medium in Ed Ruscha's prints, and vegetable dye on snails' tails in the etchings of Alice Maher. Geology is the point of departure for Tania Kovats in her drawings based on the outlines of the islands around the coast of Britain – an exposure to natural formations that plays with the gulf between spontaneous gesture and methodical transposition.

By contrast, Richard Long's drawings made by dripping and splashing River Avon mud onto black card allow an intuitive response to the accidental effects of nature. And chance and control vie for prominence in Ian Davenport's use of syringes to drip brightly coloured paint in delicate lines down the page, and in the explosive impact of Anna Barriball's thrown rubber balls coated with graphite. The slippage and uncertainty inherent in indirect methods of mark-making is exploited by Mona Hatoum in her *frottages* made from the impressions of culinary utensils and in Cornelia Parker's 'Rorschach' drawings.

The distressed photographs produced by Steven Pippin reflect the tussle between the machine and the inappropriateness of the purpose to which it is put. In Jem Finer's drawing machine, a chart recorder is transformed so that the pen records the electrical fluctuations of a detuned radio: 'The universe is permeated by radiation – the Cosmic Microwave Background – which according to contemporary cosmology is the cooled remnant of the Big Bang. It is audible all the time in the hiss of static of a radio.' Thus, the random interference in *You'll Never Know* ranges from microcosm to macrocosm, from the tiniest particles of dust to the origins of the universe.

Roger Malbert, Senior Curator, Hayward Gallery Touring
Susan May, Acting Director, Hayward Gallery Touring

NOTES ON THE AUTHORS

James Flint is the author of three novels, *Habitus* (whose characters were developed according to three different theories of chance), *52 Ways to Magic America* and *The Book of Ash*. He has written for many newspapers and magazines and for a time worked as science editor of the technology and art periodical *Mute*. Janna Levin is Professor of Physics and Astronomy at Columbia University, in New York. Her work focuses on theories of the early universe, chaos and black holes. She is the author of the popular science book *How the Universe got its Spots*, and her second book, a novel, *A Madman Dreams of Turing Machines*, is published in 2006. Sally O'Reilly is a freelance writer and critic. She writes for *Art Monthly*, *Frieze*, *Contemporary*, *Modern Painters* and *Time Out* and numerous international exhibition catalogues. She is the co-editor of *Implicasphere* and is currently devising a touring theatrical production and programming performances for the 2006 Whitstable Biennale.

Chance is a role that providence has reserved for itself in the affairs of the world, a role through which it could make certain that men would have no influence. _ JOSEPH JOUBERT

dust particles as they are disturbed by
draughts and human movement

ABOUT RANDOMNESS

A conversation between Jeni Walwin and Henry Krokatsis

Jeni Walwin: This book has grown out of an exhibition looking at ways in which artists set up structures or systems for drawing, which at a crucial moment in the process are subject to 'random interference' from an outside influence. The resulting works escape from the confines of their initial methodology by an action, usually externally generated, that plays a part in creating the final image. In many instances artists are attracted to the notion of indirect mark-making, and they move away from the work, relinquishing overall control of the final composition. We took these ideas as a starting point and looked at the ways in which chance and control jockey for position within many artists' work. Interest in these processes as a means of creating an image is not new. We set out to explore the connections between contemporary work and earlier examples from both Western and Eastern cultures where artists have deliberately exposed their work to chance elements.

Henry Krokatsis: This aleatoric approach isn't unique to the practice of art. Chance doesn't recognise boundaries; whatever activity you are engaged in, be it art, science, gambling or daily life, you can't cut it out of the equation. Creating an image by harnessing chance engenders the same feeling as waiting for your number to come up on the roulette wheel. Chance operates today just as it did a thousand years ago. This book briefly explores the place of chance in other areas of life and extends the ideas beyond visual art.

JW: We have particularly considered the impact of chance on the process of creating an image and the initial inspiration for this came from conversations with you about your own working methods as an artist. I'm thinking of your smoke drawings in particular – these works allow chance to play a significant part in determining the final image. Can you say something about how your interest in this process developed?

HK: I've always employed a strategy, in one form or another, to skip past the limits of logic or common sense; these are barriers that have to be bypassed in some way if you want to trade beyond your experience. The processes that I use aren't linear – they are pragmatic. If the method gives you the scope to deal with your line of enquiry then it's legitimate. The first time I became aware of the idea of using a process to bypass the rational was probably at nursery school. We were given a sheet of black sugar paper; I dipped some string in paint and laid it on the paper. The paper was folded in half, sandwiching the string, the lights were turned off and I pulled the string. I remember very clearly the lights going on and unfolding the paper to reveal a beautiful, perfectly symmetrical, blurred Rorschach-type image. Somehow this magical thing had emerged and I'd been involved in making it.

JW: Why would an artist today want to establish an exposure to chance?

HK: You set up a system to free yourself from the ego in order to procure the unexpected, which you hope is more relevant, more universal, than anything you could achieve through the conceptual conscious mind alone. In Buddhist thought, the strategy – the *Dharma* (the path) – leads you to understanding *Dharmata* (the inherent nature of everything). In *hoboku* (flung ink) drawings of the fifteenth and sixteenth centuries, the Cha'an Buddhist throws ink in order to make an image that breaks free from the subject that controls it. These are some of the most extraordinary images I have seen. But chance is only one strategy for escaping the preconceived image and opening up a field of transformation. You could take a shed-load of drugs and chuck some paint around. I've seen a fair amount of work made this way and apart from Henri Michaux it's generally pretty dreadful. Randomness for its own sake is not interesting. It's the right kind of randomness – the kind that resonates in a relevant way and how you position yourself to allow for it – that's important.

JW: For each artist this operates in a different way. The ability to open up to chance is triggered by a personal desire to set something in motion. Although we have been looking particularly at drawings, the mark of a pencil is rarely found in any of the works that we have selected. Artists have adopted a fantastically rich range of strategies in order to create an image that might finally be described as a drawing. Syringes, snails, mechanical toys, the wind, the sun, smoke, fire, mud, wax impressions of things, Rorschach tests, food, rust, dust, live film footage, GPS tracking devices, lit fuses, trees, washing machines, and low-tech, purpose-built contraptions have all been recruited to generate the unexpected. In each case the artist has a precise and carefully articulated reason for adopting these processes, but their real interest in using them is their attraction to the unknown, their potential for submitting to the unexpected, and to abandoning

[15]

themselves in some small way to an experience beyond their control.

HK: Do you believe in the idea of being 'on a roll'?

JW: The randomness we are talking about – that sense of being open to the roll – can only be experienced if it is accompanied by a heightened sense of purpose, by a sensitive awareness of the potential for change, and by a fierce desire to move beyond what is immediately apparent. This is not the territory of a hedonist. These moments arrive when all intellectual endeavour has been exhausted and with the realisation that by opening up to the flow of possibilities there will be a receptive response to whatever is beyond the horizon. Being 'on a roll' is surely possible, but it's necessary to recognise the ability to experience it first.

Chance opened up perceptions to me, immediate spiritual insights. Intuition led me to revere the law of chance as the highest and deepest of laws, the law that rises from the fundament. _ JEAN ARP

contact print from original negative
developed and exposed in a Wascomat
Senior w125 triple loader

HOW TO CURE A BAD CASE OF CHANCE
James Flint

*'Most people don't believe in telepathy. But then most
people have never won a World Poker Tournament
gold bracelet.'* DOYLE BRUNSON

The law of probability is strange. It seems to have a hole in it,
a logical gap that stops the two common sense ends from
meeting in a coherent middle.

Say I throw a die. There's a one in six possibility of any
number from one to six coming up. That much seems obvious.
Say I throw a six, and then I throw again. The second dice
throw is an event that is, in any practical sense, entirely discrete
from the first.

According to the law of probability there's as much chance
of a six coming up a second time as any other number. I am
after all standing on the surface of a planet, a planet that has
revolved a little further around its sun. The universe has very
slightly shifted its configuration, all around me people are
living, breathing, dying, being born. Assuming I'm not cheating,
not playing with loaded dice, this dice throw bears no relation
to the previous.

But what if I've a lot of money riding on this second
throw? What if I've bet ten thousand pounds that I can throw
two sixes in a row? That changes everything. Now the chances
of my throwing that second six are not one in six but one in
six times one in six, i.e. one in thirty-six. The only thing that's
changed is my intention. But as a result, chance has taken on

a very different shape. By yoking the two throws together in this way, in the eyes of probability I have, in effect, created a single event out of two separate components.

What this suggests is that chance operates within the fence we throw around it. Outside of that fence, the concept of chance is, in fact, meaningless. To say that everything in the universe happens by total chance is to say nothing at all. Everything is random, everything is preordained: both expressions are equally meaningless. On the subatomic level, the universe glows and pulses in giant knots and fields, behaving in ways that stretch our fancy ape brains to the limit. On the superatomic level, the level on which we live and operate, the universe is full of causal chains. Over some of these chains we have approximate and limited control; over most of them we have none at all, or very little. Chance occurs when a number of these chains, hitherto more or less discrete, collide in a way that we in some way regard as meaningful.

This is what we mean by *coincidence*. Co-incidence. Two or more things happening at the same time, in the same place. All life is produced and maintained by the coincidence of multiple causal chains, and most of these coincidences – from the interactions of sunshine and plant DNA producing an atmosphere suitable for the evolution of mammalian respiration to the miraculous appearance of our colleagues every morning at our place of work – are so habitual and repetitive that we rarely give them a second thought. Occasionally, however, a coincidence with the power to bump us from our normal routine will take place. The greater the bump, the greater the meaning and the greater – and more remarkable – the coincidence.

Casinos are specifically designed in order to create the possibility for such coincidences to occur. They are, if you like, traps for chance – and as such they're also traps for those who haven't thought clearly about chance, about how it works and the role it plays. Specific causal events – which card will be turned over next, in which socket of a spinning wheel will a bouncing ivory ball come to rest – are created with as few causally predictable precedents as possible, giving no clue as to what happens next.

Yet these events are contained within a larger causal structure, limited by there being only 52 cards in a deck, 36 numbers on a wheel. Given these restrictions, along with the others imposed by the house, we realise that while, for the player, the chance events counted as important may happen on a single play or across a single evening, the casino is operating on a wholly different time-scale, in effect an abstract one. While at any single point in time an individual player may be winning, the operations of chance are entirely contained by the abstract frame. The results, in the long run, are therefore completely predictable: that the casino, for example, will win at blackjack with an edge of two per cent, and at roulette with an edge of five per cent.

The players, of course, only observe these causal inter-actions through a small window, the one they see when they're playing. The owners see the entire operation, and understand that chance has been harnessed and domesticated. On the gaming floor chance blazes with the power of a firestorm, sucking up the oxygen and driving all before it. From the vantage point of the offices, however, it crackles with all the cosiness and reassurance of logs burning merrily in a grate. It's all a question of scale.

But there is something else, something else on the player's side, something less well understood. When confronted with the play of these short, unpredictable causal chains, chains that seem to have been divorced from any meaningful sense of causality at all, the human brain does something odd.

It goes a little crazy.

It appears that exposure to this kind of chance produces in us a narcotic effect. Our everyday ability to predict and perceive the immediate future, to form causal connections, a fairly advanced intellectual ability we pretty much take for granted and rely upon to get us through the day, is suddenly stymied. Unable to function, it becomes confused. The result is usually a combination of disorientation, euphoria and sudden superstition, understood as the creation of arbitrary meaning. Without reason dictating events, different, more fundamental parts of the brain rise to the fore: instinctual elements that are more usually dominant when our hormones are raging and fundamental appetites of hunger, power or sex are making insistent demands on our time and attention.

The rush of gambling, not unlike the rush of alcohol, is the rush of release. Inasmuch as the self is defined as the rational map that links and overlays our various bodily systems, allowing us to engage and disengage them with some level of conscious feedback, and inasmuch as consciousness itself *is* just this process of feedback in operation, the experience of gambling – of chance – entails a loss of self.

This can be a dangerous process, to be sure, but it can also be highly desirable – and not just as a source of escape from the confines of sober living. Rationality and control are only part of what makes us who we are. By putting ourselves in situations where rationality is forced to give way to instinct

– a process that philosophers call *ecstasis* – we can learn more about who we are and why we react to things the way we do. It's a kind of transformation, and with the transformation of ourselves the world around us changes too. No longer do we see it as a collection of more or less stable systems that can be negotiated more or less predictably. Instead it becomes a formless and chaotic zone, one in which we have to learn to trust our instincts. If we manage this, and if our instincts prove at all reliable, we soon find ourselves experiencing the extraordinary sensation of being in touch with the universe – with being, if you like – in a far more intimate way than our rational faculties ever manage to effect.

With drugs and casino games, this feeling of ecstasis, of being in touch with things, of being 'on a roll', is – sadly – utterly illusory. But in situations in which we find ourselves involved with natural systems or other human beings – in sports, or the arts, or in games where psychology and animal reaction plays a role equal or greater than that of chance – these instincts can serve us better than any system of logic. Through them we call on the extraordinary resources of the deeper neural structures of our brains, structures that have been honed by a combination of evolved architecture and lived experience to interface with the world almost seamlessly.

When this happens, it's as if we've inserted ourselves into a causal chain. In so doing we are relinquishing our perception that the world is happening *to* us and accepting that we are inside of it, part of it: not watching from the bank but standing in the river, as Zen disciples like to say. In other words we are *becoming coincidence*: we are co-inciding with events around us, the irony being that these moments of sublimation, during which we give over our egos and subject ourselves absolutely to the greater forces around us, to the 'will of the world', are at the time likely to be the only moments in our lives when we feel absolute freedom, that we could do anything we wanted to at all.

This paradoxical feeling, experienced at exactly these moments, is what we call joy.

Oh heaven over the pure and high! Now that I have learned that there is no purposeful external spider and no spider web of reason, you have become for me a dance floor for Divine accidents. _ZARATHUSTRA

paint syringed down paper in
uncontrolled vertical lines

QUANTUM CHANCE
Janna Levin

A painter flicks paint from her brush and thinks it is up to
chance where the drops will stick. A filmmaker throws a
camera out of a window and collects the random frames.
A sculptor arranges fruit to rot and leaves the rest to chance.
But there is no chance in a mechanistic world where paint
is a fluid that drips under gravity's pull and light reacts with
resin and organic matter rots to chemicals and air. There is
no chance.

There are factors outside of our control, beyond our
ability to decipher or to know. There are accidents and
mistakes. There is chaos and disorder, but these labels
describe our human shortcomings, our inability to manage
all the details, our eyes' reliance on pattern and our minds'
reliance on order. In all of nature, there is no such thing
as chance.

Not even in the throw of the dice. There are just too
many factors to track. There are subtle forces out of human
control but not out of the universe's control. I throw a pair
of dice slightly high, with an intentional spin and a prepara-
tory rattle. But I'm not so in control of my motor functions
that I can be certain exactly how high, how torqued, how
scrambled they are before they fall. I throw them into the air
and a bath of moving molecules jostle the cubes until they
land on an imperfect surface, bounce and settle. An eight.
I throw an eight. It seems random but it's not. That eight
(a six plus a two) was determined inevitably the moment the
universe was created. Every event in the universe is caused
by some preceding event, which in turn is caused by some

preceding event. The succession of cause and effect can be traced back to the Big Bang itself. All the particles in all the world were set into motion, along fixed orbits through fourteen billion years of cosmic evolution until our galaxy formed, our sun, our planet, DNA, our species, plastics, casinos, this pair of dice, these hands, this throw. An eight.

In principle, all the atoms in the entire cosmos could be followed, their orbits traced throughout history, and a map of all the future made. The fate of civilization already encoded in the landscape in the moment of creation. Our motion through time toward that fixed future is an illusory ride along complex tracks. Our own participation so convincingly free but that very freedom is a trick of the mind, a cunning of the code.

In a purely mechanistic, deterministic world, there can be no such thing as free choice. Our atoms, our neurons, our brains, our thoughts, our desires, our beliefs are all reducible to forces – to actions and reactions, to cause and effect, just like the dice. When a painter makes a mark on the page they believe it to be a consequence of their intention. When paint splashes, it seems a consequence of chance. Yet both human intention and the splatter of a drop are inescapable steps in a deterministic, mechanistic reality. Intention and chance are not so different.

At least this is what thousands of years of human experience and scientific experiment seemed to imply. The world appeared strictly deterministic. Rigidly causal. But then scientists discovered quantum mechanics, the physics of sub-atomic particles. With great resistance and outright disbelief, scientists began to uncover, to measure, and to quantify chance. Chance in the very fabric of reality.

I look at a little white die and it seems so real, so concrete, so solid. But it might not be any of these things. If you magnified the die to an atomic level, you would find it is composed of atoms, each with a core nucleus orbited by satellite electrons. The rest of the cube is empty space. When you try to hone in on the electrons, they appear to be infinitesimal point particles but under closer inspection their location and their motion cannot be determined with unlimited precision. They are waves. They are particles. They are both, mutually exclusively. They are impossible. Yet there they are in experiment after experiment. Present if impossible to pinpoint. When we look for them we find them whole − indivisible. Each electron a perfect reproduction of every other.

In some sense, the electron does not exist. There are only waves of probability. All that exists is chance − a chance that the electron is here or there. A chance with a certain probability. There is a famous experiment known as the double slit experiment. A beam of electrons (or, in the case of the original experiment, a beam of light) is shone on a barrier with two open slits. The electrons pass through the slits and interfere on the other side of the barrier to create an interference pattern. Mathematically, only a wave could produce such an interference pattern. Even if you arrange for only one particle at a time to reach the barrier, the interference pattern still emerges, as though each individual electron is a wave that interferes with itself − a wave that passes through both slits at once and sloshes together again on the other side. Except an electron is indivisible. It cannot smear out. It cannot pass through both slits at once. It is as though the electron doesn't really exist, only the probability of detecting an electron exists. Chance is a wave that can pass through both slits at once.

[29]

If this sounds contradictory it is only because it is contradictory. A particle cannot be a wave. But it is. Matter should exist at a certain place or not. But matter does both simultaneously. There should be no chance. But there is. Einstein rejected quantum mechanics for this very reason with the oft-quoted quip, 'God does not play dice'. Unless God does.

Quantum mechanics isn't just a fantasy about the microscopic world. It works like a perfect key to a previously sealed door. The predictions from quantum mechanics are accurate to remarkable precision. Even so, it is only with bewilderment that we concede what we can't quite grasp intellectually – that matter is elusive, that there really is chance.

As we are composites of electrons and other elementary particles, quantum chance plays some part in the lives we act out on nearly (but not entirely) fixed orbits in a probabilistic universe that has some chance of being born. When I look at marks on a canvas, frames in a film, the arrangements of an installation, I can only wonder how much was really up to chance.

We have had enough of the considered actions that have swollen beyond measure our credulity in the blessings of science. What we want now is 'spontaneity' not because it is more beautiful or better than anything else. But because everything that comes from us freely without intervention from speculative ideas represents us. _ TRISTAN TZARA

drawing pens attached to the outer
branches of a larch tree

FROM CHAOS TO ORDER AND BACK AGAIN
Sally O'Reilly

Chance and control need not be antagonistic. The drip of paint
can live happily next to the neat border; wild irresponsibility
in one aspect of life might actually be supported by caution in
another. Artists have suspected this for some time. From the
Renaissance onwards controlling devices, such as perspective,
were formulated to push the painted image closer and closer
to an illusion of reality. There were incidents along the way,
however, that proved in retrospect to short-circuit reason and
create innovative breakthroughs – they were serendipitous
moments when chaos encroached onto order, whether by
accident or invitation.

During the late nineteenth century an emphasis on painterly
qualities emerged in Europe. The Impressionists, for instance,
encouraged paint to be itself, as well as describe an object.
You could say that there was a switch of emphasis from the
pictured to the picture, or the painted to the paint itself. Artists
since have developed this tendency to almost ludicrous lengths,
and there are artworks that pivot entirely on the splashes and
smears of accident. Gutai, for example, the Japanese group of
the 1950s and 1960s, transformed painting into a technique
that involved the whole body. They wallowed in paint, supine
on the floor, jumped through big sheets of paper and shot paint
from a canon, liberating mark-making from the self-conscious,
finicky hand of the tentative artist.

As well as the invitation of the visceral into process,
there are also artists who consciously decide to relinquish an
artwork to unknown forces – call it fate, statistics, God's will
or whatever. Marcel Duchamp is often identified as the point

[33]

from which this evolved, when he dropped a one-metre length of string onto the floor three times, recording its curve each time in a template. These forms, called *Three Standard Stoppages* (1913–14), were later used in formulating other works, such as his *Large Glass* (1914–23). Through this experiment, Duchamp was not only purposefully inviting the influence of external forces, but also suggesting that our scientific obsession with measuring is easily displaced by chaotic forces such as gravity. We rarely encounter an entirely straight edge – his curves are far more probable. It could be said, then, that experiment is more representative of our experience in the universe than any composed picture. How much more evocative of a slap in the face is a violent paint spillage than a static drawing of the act? It is this turning point, from representation to demonstration, which has enlivened art of the last century. Compare a painting by Edward Hopper, where the ennui of middle America is almost palpable in the deserted scenes of mediocrity, with a performance that might last hours or even days, the boredom crashing over you in waves as you inwardly beg for the end. But this is not to announce the art object as irrelevant or somehow ineffectual in communicating what it is to be human. A painting or sculpture, although motionless, is not inert. It can serve as evidence of an action; we can empathise with how it was made and imagine the narrative of its materialisation.

Sometimes we are afforded the luxury of enjoying a leisurely drive instead of rushing to a destination. Process-based art is analogous to this: the mode of materialisation is priori-tised over the outcome. It could even be that an artist embarks on a piece without any idea of what the outcome might be, so that the point of arrival creeps up or jumps out from a blind alley along the way. During the 1970s, the conceptual photographer Douglas Huebler set himself tasks, such as every five minutes snapping pictures of the first mannequin he laid eyes on in London's Oxford Street; the results would then be framed and presented along with the instructions that produced them. This is counter to a pre-twentieth century image of the tortured artist questing for perfection but, to the relief of many artists, it needn't be like this any more. Many encourage the unexpected during the journey; they enjoy overcoming problems, negotiating new parameters or assimilating other individuals or societies. Artist Sophie Calle constructs encounters with strangers, perhaps following someone to another country or inviting people to sleep in her bed. Who knows where such experiences might lead?

The traditional artist might have complained of this as a loss of control, but there are many ways to invite positive intrusion. You can allow physical forces, like gravity or the weather, a free rein. Or you can invite the influence of another's will – the general public, another artist or an animal. Or you can test your ability to follow your own instructions in a display of stamina or quick thinking or subconscious associations. I wondered if I could find a way of illustrating this through the writing of this essay, instead of simply describing its occurrence elsewhere. Instead of writing about a series of decisions made by artists throwing dice, perhaps I could pick words from, say, an art history book using the same method. You can probably imagine though that this would be neither enlightening nor interesting. There is something about visual art that allows chance to enrich it, whereas in writing the fundamental process of stringing words together must be sensible. The joy of Dada poetry, made up of cut-out words pulled from a bag, arguably lies entirely in the concept, rarely in the stream of surreal but ultimately meaningless language. And this is the nub: meaning attaches itself to the written or spoken word with grimmer shackles than it does to an image or an abstract idea.

Artists are aware that by opening the floodgates to chance they are not necessarily closing the door on sense or sensibility. The question is whether we can carry this across into life. Can we remind ourselves that, although we may appear to be in the driving seat, we are not really in control; we are not authoring our autobiographies as we go? Lived life is not as rational as language and, if we take a random route to work instead of the most efficient one, we may well see something wonderful or we might be flattened by a lorry. This is the risk that we court, but it should be remembered that to take a chance and make an opportunity are indeed closely linked; they might be separated for safety's sake, or one could be converted to the other, but they are rarely far apart. Managing, worrying, controlling, failing, reasoning, flourishing – these words smack of nasty managerial jargon, but they are verbs we perform in our daily fight to control chaos. No longer are art and life about the imperious divination of reason and truth – success is something much more random and altogether messier.

*When I wrote the 'Imaginary Landscapes' for twelve radios,
it was not for the purpose of shock or as a joke but rather to
increase the unpredictability already inherent in the situation
through the tossing of coins. Chance, to be precise, is a leap,
provides a leap out of reach of one's own grasp of oneself.
Once done, forgotten.* _ JOHN CAGE

drawing with a lit fuse

NOTES ON THE PROCESSES

These notes describe the processes used by the artists in making the works illustrated on the following pages (in order of appearance):

Hermann Rorschach
Inkblot created by Swiss psychiatrist Hermann Rorschach as a test for psychopathological projection. Published as one of a set of cards in 1921.

Mona Hatoum
Rubbed impressions of culinary objects on Japanese wax paper.

Rebecca Horn
Drawing produced by the ritualised turning of the head back and forth.

Richard Long
River Avon mud dripped onto card.

Ed Ruscha
One of a series of screen prints using food and other organic materials, in this case axel grease and caviar, on Silver snow white antique finish paper.

John Wood and Paul Harrison
Thirty-six actions recorded from a fixed camera position in the centre of a specially constructed ceilingless box room.

Henry Krokatsis
Fire-proofed stencils held over burning rags allowing carbon deposits to collect onto paper above.

Jem Finer
A chart recorder is transformed into an automatic drawing machine, its source the electrical fluctuations of a detuned radio. The universe is permeated by radiation, the Cosmic Microwave Background, which contemporary cosmology concludes is the cooled remnant of the Big Bang. Everywhere, all the time, it's visible in the snow between channels on a television, the hiss of static on a radio, the rattling pen of the chart recorder, like a spirit hand.

Anna Barriball
One of a series of drawings where a rubber ball covered with graphite is thrown onto paper.

Alice Maher
Traces of vegetable dye applied to snails' tails, combined with the artist's own compositions to create a series of five etchings.

Tim Knowles
Artist's drawing pens are attached to the outer branches of a larch tree in Borrowdale, Cumbria. A sheet of paper is placed on an easel beneath them and the movement of wind in the tree creates the drawing. One of a series using different trees, the character of each tree (willow, hawthorn, birch, beach, oak) is evoked by the marks made.

Steven Pippin

Contact print from original negative developed and exposed in a Wascomat Senior w125 triple loader. From a series created in a laundromat, the washing machine operating as both pinhole camera and (by applying developing fluids through the soap dispenser) as darkroom. Mr Pippin observes that 'the chemical process is virtually identical in photography and laundry. The action of bleach drives out anything dark or black in order to make it white or transparent.'

Dave Farnham

Film of a drawing in which a lit fuse traces the interior structure of the artist's studio. The resulting film is then shown in negative so that the white flare becomes black and the darkened studio white.

Keith Tyson

'The Artmachine is a complex algorithm, a step-by-step computational rule, which has been specifically designed to generate proposals for an endless number of artworks. It treats the world as a giant database ... It makes decisions about every aspect of form and content ... Tyson decodes the Artmachine's coded specifications and then physically realises the given artwork or "iteration".' Kate Bush

Ian Davenport

Coloured paint applied with syringes and allowed to drop down a sheet of paper in uncontrolled vertical lines.

Claude Heath
Blindfolded, the artist with one hand feels the head of a small sculpture of the Buddha, whilst the other hand renders the sensations in a drawing.

Anne Bean
A drawing made outdoors over the course of a year. A sheet of paper is fixed to the wall with a small globe suspended in front of it. The shadows cast on the paper are traced in a different colour for each month of the year.

Tania Kovats
The artist traces the outlines of the islands around Britain to scale on matt film paper, filling them in and layering them in groups up to six deep.

Damien Roach
Live film installation of a brightly-lit area of the gallery floor revealing dust particles as they are disturbed by draughts and human movement.

Stephen Cripps
Drawing for a performance, showing film projected physically (i.e. not taken up by a second spool) and ignited by flames from a gas cylinder below. Cripps made drawings to explore performance ideas and to record traces of past performances.

Cornelia Parker
'Rorschach' drawing made with Ferric Oxide from a pornographic videotape confiscated by HM Customs & Excise, suspended in solvent.

Chance baffles its way through man's unconscious.
_ ANDRÉ BRETON

PICTURE CREDITS

ACKNOWLEDGEMENTS

In addition to all the artists listed on p.47, the curators and the Hayward Gallery would like to thank the following for their help in realising this project: Judy Adam, Jade Awdry, Geock Brown, Eleanor Bryson, Steve Bullas, Tim Clark, James Dalrymple, Kerry Duggan, Sian Ede, Helen Faulkner, Jonathan Harvey, Patrick Heide, Sophie Higgs, Pernilla Holmes, Bernard Jacobson, Mark King, Jeremy Lewison, Alice Lobb, Helen Luckett, Alison Maun, Kate Murray, David Risley, Soraya Rodriguez, Nick Rogers, Julian Rothenstein, Charlotte Schepke, Nichola Shane, Felicity Sparrow, Adrian Sutton, Daniella Valle, Richard Walkley, Alister Warman, and Caroline Wetherilt.

The exhibition was organised in its initial stages by Jacky Klein and Rachel Kent. We would also like to thank our colleagues at the exhibiting venues, including Lindsay Taylor and Richard Smith at the Harris Museum and Art Gallery, Preston; Jenni Spencer-Davies and Karen MacKinnon at the Glynn Vivian Art Gallery, Swansea; Mark Doyle at The Lowry, Salford; Stephen Snoddy and Deborah Robinson at the New Art Gallery, Walsall; and Fiona Venables at Tullie House Museum and Art Gallery, Carlisle.

ARTISTS IN THE EXHIBITION

Anna Barriball
Anne Bean
Ian Breakwell
Paul Cassidy
Stephen Cripps
Layla Curtis
Ian Davenport
Tracey Emin
Dave Farnham
Jem Finer
Peter Fischli and David Weiss
Mona Hatoum
Claude Heath
Rebecca Horn
Tim Knowles
Tania Kovats
Henry Krokatsis
Richard Long
Alice Maher
Cornelia Parker
Steven Pippin
Damien Roach
Ed Ruscha
Keir Smith
Keith Tyson
Mark Wallinger
Klaus Weber
John Wood and Paul Harrison

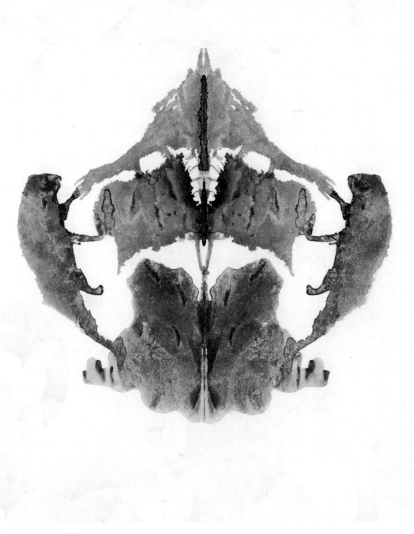

Hermann Rorschach
Inkblot, c. 1921

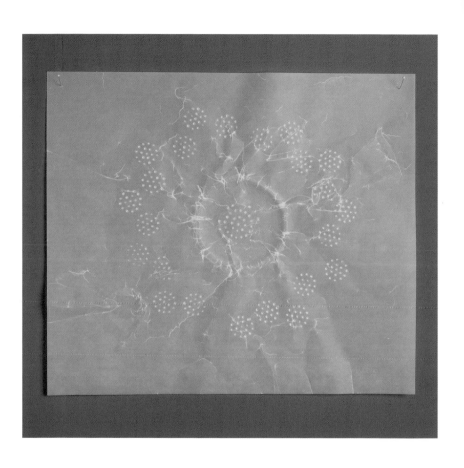

Mona Hatoum
Untitled (râpe cylindrique), 1999
Japanese wax paper

Rebecca Horn
Pencil Mask, 1972 (still)
DVD

Richard Long
Untitled, 2005
River Avon mud on black card

Ed Ruscha
Brews, 1970
Organic screen print on paper

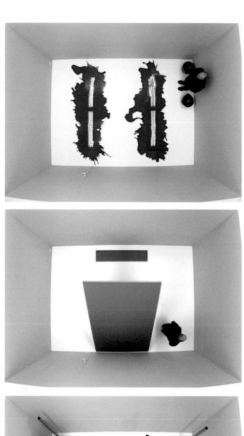
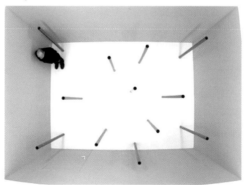

John Wood and Paul Harrison
Hundredweight, 2003 (stills)
6-monitor DVD installation

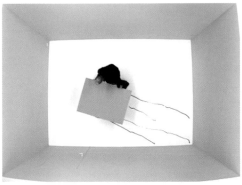

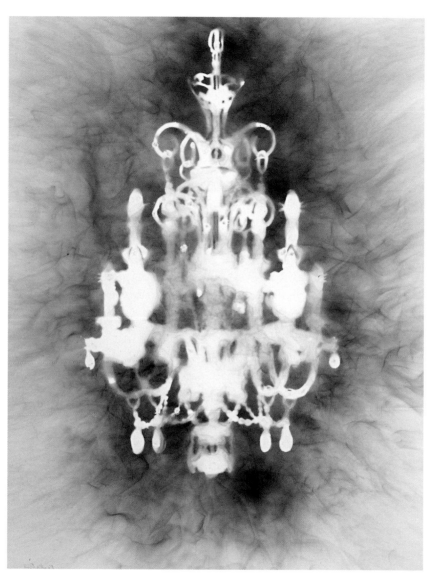

Henry Krokatsis
Chandelier 1, 2003
Carbon deposit on paper

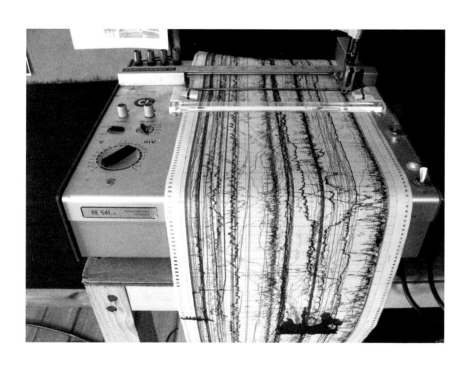

Jem Finer
Everywhere, All the Time, 2005
Digital IR

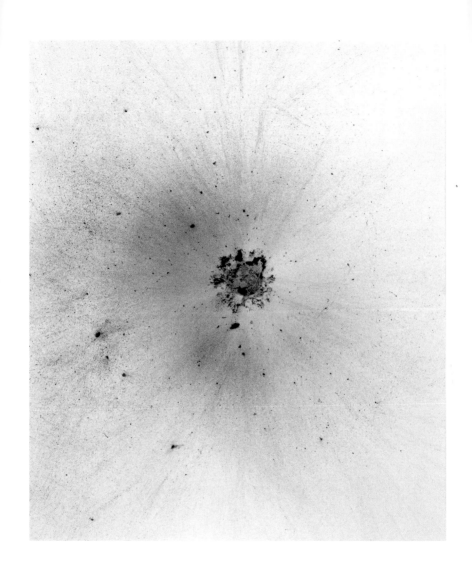

Anna Barriball
14:03:27, 2002
Graphite powder on paper

Alice Maher
Helix Virginius, 2004
From *The Snail Chronicles*
Set of 5 etchings

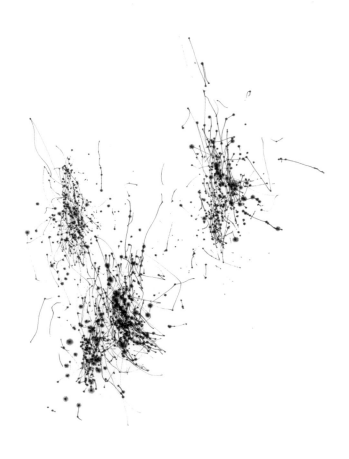

Tim Knowles
Tree Drawing – Larch on easel [4 pen] # 1, 27/06/2005
Photograph and ink on paper

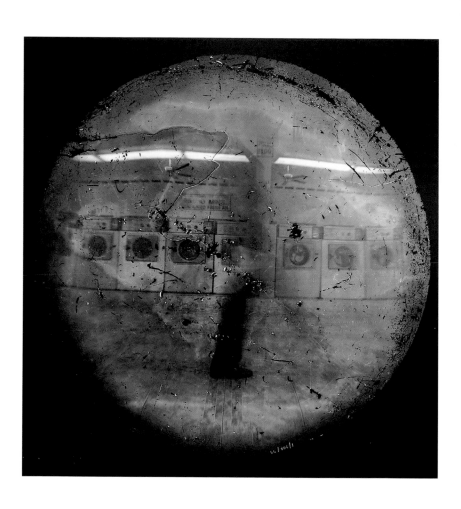

Steven Pippin
Laundromat / Locomotion, 1997
Photograph

Dave Farnham
Untitled, 2003 (still)
DVD projection

Iteration :	AMCHII• XV		**Size / Duration :**	150 x 250 cm diameter
Title :	Timemachine *(For travelling into the future at a rate of 9 192 631 770 periods of the radiation corresponding to the transition between 2 hyperfine levels of the ground state of a caesium–133 atom per second.)*		**Untitled number :**	•
			Series & Editions :	Unique
			Hanging Specs. :	Floor
			Location / Site :	Any
Format :	Sculpture		**Documentation :**	•
			Date :	1995
			Conditions :	•
Status :	Proposed		**Other variables :**	•

Brief description of proposed work / Reproduction of finished work

A) TIMEMACHINE
B) FIBREGLASS CASES • C) FIBRE GLASS HEAD UNIT • D) AERI-
AL • E) POWER UNIT • F) WOOD & FABRIC UNIT • G) WOOD &
ALL. UNIT • H) REST UNIT WITH DIGITAL DISPLAY • I) WOOD,
PLASTIC & ELECTRONIC CONTROL UNIT • J) BASE LIGHTS •
L) PIPE • M) MDF BASE.

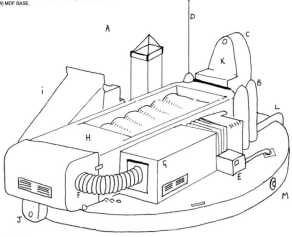

Notes : This Machine actually travels at the specified rate into the future, but as all things travel at this rate*, its function is more meditative than transportive, isolating the temporal experience rather than accelerating it. A fusion of a sculpture and a time based piece (the long title is the scientific definition of a second after the original definition of: " 1 / 86 400 of the mean solar day" was considered too inaccurate to keep). *(With all the clauses of relativity aside.)

Iteration :	AMCHII• XXXIX		Size / Duration :	apprx.150 x 180 x 75 cm
Title :	Hammerhead Flamingo		Untitled number :	•
			Series & Editions :	Unique
			Hanging Specs. :	Floor
			Location / Site :	•
Format :	Sculpture		Documentation :	•
			Date :	1995
			Conditions :	Lit from below
Status :	Proposed		Other variables :	•

Brief description of proposed work / Reproduction of finished work

AMCHII•XXXIX
"Hammerhead Flamingo"

Notes :
This rubber and plastic sculpture stands on a circular lightbox as the piece needs to be lit from below, therefore, the piece should be exhibited in a dark or dimly lit space.

Keith Tyson
100 Original Artmachine Iteration Sheets, 1994–95 (details)
Ink on paper, photographs, felt tip pen

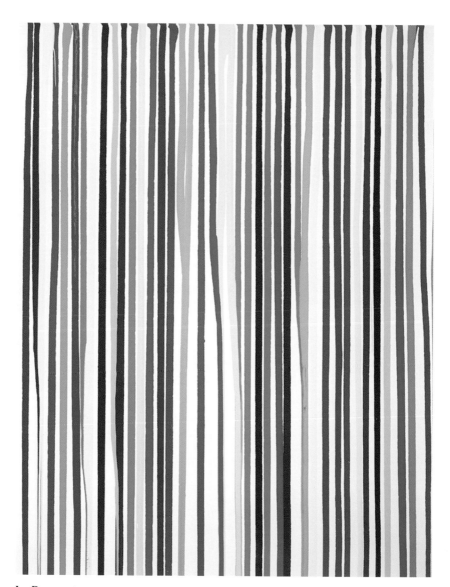

Ian Davenport
Poured paints: ice white, 2003
Water-based paint on paper

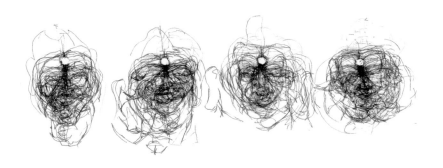

Claude Heath
Buddha − Drawing 102, 1995
Red, green and black biro ink on paper

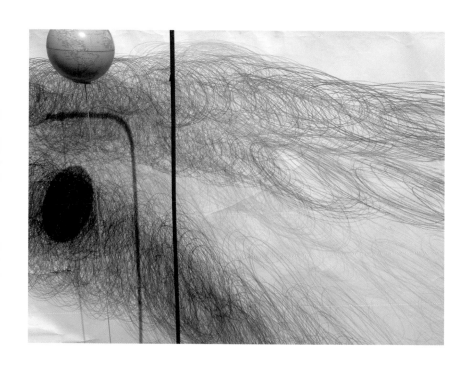

Anne Bean
ECLIPSE, September 2004 – September 2005 (detail, work in progress)
Coloured pencil on paper

Tania Kovats
'The British isles', 2003 (detail)
Ink on film paper

Damien Roach
A Small Big Thing, 2003 (installation shot)
Mixed media installation

Stephen Cripps
Untitled, 1977
Ink, glue and charcoal on paper

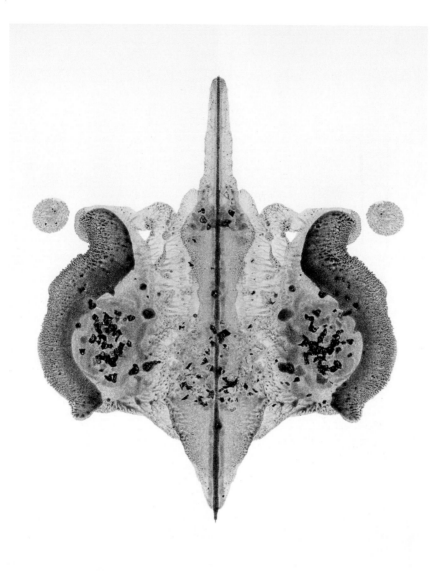

Cornelia Parker
Drawing made with Ferric Oxide from a pornographic video tape suspended in solvent (confiscated by HM Customs & Excise), 1997